A GUIDE FOR

DEVELOPING AND

CONTROLLING

INFORMANTS

Michael E. Grimes

LawTech Publishing Co., Ltd.

A Guide for Developing and Controlling
INFORMANTS

Published by:

LawTech Publishing Co., Ltd.

1060 Calle Cordillera, Ste. 105

San Clemente, CA 92673

1(949) 498-4815

FAX: 1(949) 498-4858

website: www.lawtech-pub.com or www.lawtech.cc

Printed in the USA

p. 88

ISBN: 1-930466-12-9

ABOUT THE AUTHOR

Michael E. Grimes spent 28 years with the United States Department of Justice in law enforcement. He began his career with the Bureau of Narcotics and Dangerous Drugs and continued as a Special Agent when the organization became the Drug Enforcement Administration. He spent his entire career either working in the field as an agent or supervising field agents. As an agent and as a supervisor he dealt with hundreds of informants and saw most, if not all, mistakes that can be made by law enforcement officers in dealing with informants. In 1980, Agent Grimes began sharing his observations with other law enforcement officers and has since lectured extensively to federal, state, and local police officers and agents nationwide. He gratefully acknowledges the contributions of these fellow law enforcement officers in creating this manual.

ACKNOWLEDGMENT

Thank you C.J.A. for your friendship and your valuable editorial and legal assistance in the development of this guide.

TABLE OF CONTENTS

This page intentionally left blank.

INTRODUCTION

The use of informants is vital to the success of the drug enforcement operations of any law enforcement agency. Rarely can a drug case be developed without the services of informants at some stage of the investigation. This is why knowing the proper procedures for handling an informant is important for officers. The material in this manual was developed through the misfortune of many who have used informants. Use of the manual will help maintain the integrity of the department, the controlling officer, and the investigation. Police departments that do not set up and maintain a standardized system for the development and control of informants will be subject to intense scrutiny and criticism by the courts and the community.

An informant is someone who has broken a "bond." Once this occurs, there is nothing to stop him from doing it again. An informant will attack a police officer with questionable accusations if the informant views this as necessary and if given an opportunity. Officers who do not follow proper handling procedures create these opportunities. The relationship between the informant and the police becomes the first item of interest once an accusation has been made. The Rules in this manual, if followed by police officers, will help prevent this situation. This does not mean that informants will not make accusations against officers anyway. It does mean that officers who follow the Rules will clearly establish an appropriate informant relationship, which can be very useful as a defense if needed.

Because an informant is an agent of a law enforcement agency, these rules and guidelines also protect the agency from the wrongdoing of the informant. An informant cannot be watched at all times. Nevertheless, you can control your own behavior, and appropriate behavior is following rules and regulations. When a law enforcement agency sets up controls, rules, and regulations, it has done everything possible to limit culpability when an informant goes astray. Controlling informants also gives assurance to the courts that a department has done everything possible to prevent an informant from committing illegal acts.

PURPOSE OF INFORMANTS

Informants are useful for gathering information not readily available to police officers. The informant can go places and make observations where strangers (undercover or surveillance officers) would immediately be suspect. The informant can conduct undercover negotiations, have conversations with suspicious persons and obtain firsthand, timely intelligence. Therefore, the use of informants is usually a necessity and the proper, and controlled use of informants is mandatory.

When using the guidelines set forth in this manual, officers should be aware of and comply with federal, state, and local laws that may affect the use of informants. A thorough familiarity with those laws is mandatory. Where there is any conflict between those laws and this manual, the laws will always have priority. The rules in this manual are intended to help facilitate compliance with the laws.

Note, for ease of reading, the male gender is used almost exclusively throughout the text when referring to officers and informants.

This page intentionally left blank.

CHAPTER 1

THE INITIAL MEETING

UNDERSTANDING MOTIVATION

There are seven common reasons why someone decides to become an informant. No matter what the reason, his actions are usually abnormal and self-serving. The one exception to this is the "concerned citizen." A concerned citizen is someone who is cooperating with the police because he believes that what he is doing is both a moral and legal obligation to the community. The concerned citizen has no involvement in the crime.

Different motivations may need to be dealt with differently. No matter what the motivation, the informant's abnormal behavior can be turned against the police if it suits the informant's needs. Officers must recognize that an informant is someone who has broken a bond with his brethren in crime.

Motivations of Informants

Defendant/Informant

This is someone who has been charged with a crime. There is more than one potential problem here. Does the prosecuting attorney agree with a defendant cooperating with the police? Does an attorney represent the person? The informant's attorney must concur with the cooperation and will usually work out an agreement with the prosecutor. Making an agreement such as this is not within the scope of police authority. Officers of the court (attorneys) must make these agreements. An officer should never work with an informant who is represented by an attorney without the specific consent of that attorney. The prosecutor should work out the cooperation of a represented informant. If the defendant/informant is under court supervision, the court's agreement to the cooperation may be necessary. It is the officer's responsibility to report any questionable matters to the prosecuting attorney.

Mercenary

The mercenary works for money, stimulation, or other reward. He is very inclined to carry a firearm, handcuffs, or badges. Eventually, the mercenary may brag to friends about his exploits with the "government." He may tell strangers that he is a police officer and use this for some personal gain. The latter behavior is clearly illegal. Officers must guard against this because the informant may some-day say the officer knew what he was doing, or at least should have known. This problem is dealt with in the informant agreement section of this manual. Officers must conduct unannounced "pat downs" on informants, particularly the mercenary. If the mercenary or any other informant is caught with a concealed firearm, or any contraband, he must be arrested immediately and all agreements and operations terminated until the matter is resolved.

Revenge

The revenge informant works to retaliate against someone specific. He attempts to select whom he will work against and to this end the informant is not under control. Informants should never be allowed to select targets, this is police business.

Fear of Indictment

This informant is working because he believes he may be charged with a crime. If it is the intention of the government to charge this person, his cooperation must be coordinated with the prosecuting attorney. He is expecting consideration. This person may be the target of another agency and the informant may be aware of this but will not tell you.

"Reformer"

This is a person who will usually state that he wants to "clean up his life" or to "clean up the neighborhood." He usually owes another drug dealer money and will use the judicial system to liquidate the debt or he may be attempting to eliminate competition. The reformer will also want to select the targets.

Insurance

This type of informant seeks to cooperate with the police just in case he gets arrested. He is not unlike the "revenge" informant who will usually select low level dealers as the targets. He is using the police as tools. This is not acceptable.

Father/Mother Image

This person seeks strong emotional support from the controlling officer and will do whatever it takes to please the officer.

These definitions are not intended to suggest that persons with certain motivations should not be used as informants. They may all be used but with a clear recognition of the informant's motivation so that significant controls will be used to direct the informant's activities properly.

DOCUMENTING THE INFORMANT

The first step in establishing someone as an informant is to create a document file that will include fingerprints, photograph, a personal history, and any criminal record. If an informant refuses to be documented, he should not be used. Informants are to do as they are told, within the confines of the law and reason. Controlling the informant is paramount in the police officer/informant relationship. This control begins with the documentation process. It immediately alerts the informant that your department has specific procedures that must always be followed.

Fingerprints

Fingerprinting is essential to ensure that you know the informant's true identity and criminal history. The FBI indexes fingerprint cards by the fingerprint classification. So, no matter what name is on the fingerprint card, that card will be filed by fingerprint classification. A person could have been arrested several times and have given a different name each time. If that person never gives his true name, then a criminal history check using the true name will come back negative. Informants must be fingerprinted and their prints sent to the FBI for an effective criminal history check. On the front of the FD-249 fingerprint card, in the section entitled "charge," enter "criminal inquiry." The FBI will return the fingerprint card along with any criminal record. You may need these prints in the future... today's informant may be tomorrow's criminal.

Photograph

The informant photograph has many uses. It ensures identity to officers who do not know the informant. An informant has no need to observe or meet every officer, particularly officers working undercover on cases in which this informant is not involved. The undercover officer may have a need to recognize the informant. The photo can be used in place of a face to face meeting. It can also be included in lineups and in future criminal investigations where the informant may be a suspect.

Personal History

Many informants will become involved in criminal activity. They have a habit of disappearing when needed for information or for court. The personal history statement (booking information) will give officers many leads in finding the informant. It should contain the same information as a booking record.

EXAMPLE

A man was arrested for a petty crime that did not require fingerprinting. He gave a false name and other false background information that did not reveal a criminal history. The man volunteered to furnish drug information and was established as an informant. During the establishing procedure he was fingerprinted and the prints were sent to the FBI Identification Division. The man was wanted in Texas for rape and attempted murder. Had this person been used to any extent, it would have resulted in dismissing any case in which he was involved.

THE INFORMANT AGREEMENT

This may also be entitled "Code of Conduct." Every department should use a written agreement with the informant to avoid any misunderstanding about the informant's obligation to obey the law and follow regulations. This document may one day become an item of evidence should the informant decide to violate the law and use his relationship with your department as insurance against prosecution.

The agreement should be read aloud and signed by the informant in the presence of two officers who also sign as witnesses. The document should contain some or all of the following language:

1. I understand that I am not a police officer and have no authority as such. I may not arrest or search anyone, seize anything, or represent myself as a law enforcement officer. _____ (initials of informant)

2. I may not carry a badge, police credentials, or any firearm or other illegal weapon. _____

3. I will be required to consent to a search of my person or automobile anytime while working with the police as a confidential source. If this search results in the finding of illegal drugs, weapons, or other contraband, I will be prosecuted. _____

4. I will take no independent action. I understand I have no authority to engage in drug trafficking, to possess illegal drugs, make deliveries or collect money for a drug deal, unless it is performed with the specific prior consent of an officer and under the direction and control of an officer. _____

5. I am not to use illegal drugs anytime whether working undercover or not. _____

6. I am not to beg, pressure, coerce, or threaten any-one to commit a criminal act. _____

7. I am not to use sexual acts or a promise of sexual acts to induce anyone to commit a crime. _____

8. I will be required to sign statements regarding any present undercover activity or any past involve-ment in criminal activity. _____

9. I understand that no promises or representations can be made to me regarding alien status and/or my right to enter or remain in the United States. _____

10. I understand that I cannot be guaranteed any re-ward, payments, or other compensation, and I am liable for any taxes due. _____

11. I will be required to submit to questioning by pros-ecuting attorneys and may be required to testify in court. My testimony must be truthful no matter what the results. _____

12. I may be required to submit to questioning by offi-cers from another agency or department. _____

13. I may be required to submit to a polygraph exami-nation, drug urine test, or other test to ensure my credibility and effectiveness. _____

14. I understand that no promises or representations can be made to me regarding any treatment of my prior involvement in criminal activity, other than a

promise to make my cooperation known to the prosecutor and the court. _____

Informant's signature: _____

Date:_____

Witnessed by: _____

Witnessed by: _____

The informant should initial each item and the end of the document should bear the date signed, the informant's signature, and the signatures of two witnessing police officers. If a lawyer represents the person, the lawyer also must sign.

EXAMPLE

A walk-in informant wanted to furnish information about suspects transporting cocaine via private aircraft from south Florida to North Carolina. The informant was documented and required to sign an informant agreement (contract). While the informant was furnishing agents with information, he was also negotiating with an undercover agent in Oklahoma City, Oklahoma. The informant was offering the Oklahoma undercover agent several thousand pounds of marijuana for sale. The Oklahoma City agent checked agency files and determined his target was also an informant. The informant was being tape recorded by the undercover agent and his controlling agents in North Carolina. He never mentioned to his controlling agents that he was setting up a drug deal in Oklahoma and he was eventually arrested by the Oklahoma agents.

The informant's defense was based upon his cooperation with the government. He testified that he was working for the agents at the time of his arrest. The jury chose to believe the informant had double-crossed the agents and convicted him. During the trial, the informant agreement and tape recordings were introduced. They played a very important role in obtaining a conviction.

CONDUCTING THE BACKGROUND INVESTIGATION

Following the documentation process and taking an initial statement from an informant, a limited background investigation should be conducted to confirm the informant's claims to identity, residences, associates, and prior criminal activity.

Identity can be as easy as checking a photograph ID and conducting a driver's license check. Try checking the telephone book for the informant's number. If the telephone number is not listed as the informant states, you may subpoena the subscriber information. You can also check a crisscross directory and call directory assistance to confirm the number and address. Occasionally conduct a visual check of the informant's home to find out if the informant resides where you have been told, or if it appears any unusual activity takes place there.

Contact police departments that cover the area of previous residences. Seek out intelligence information that will not be available through criminal history checks. The person you are dealing with may be an informant for another agency or department as well. Or, may be the target of an ongoing investigation by another division within your department, or by another department or agency.

EXAMPLE

Many years ago in Washington, D.C., a walk-in informant wanted to furnish information and work on a big heroin case. As required, the informant was fingerprinted and photographed. In the agents' haste to make a big case they did not deliver the fingerprints to the FBI Identification Division office that was only two blocks away. The informant, who happened to be a Federal fugitive, wanted to have some fun. The agents gave the informant money to cover expenses. Approximately thirty agents from Washington, D.C., and Baltimore, MD, got involved with the informant over an entire weekend. The scheme included conducting surveillance on persons, vehicles, residences, bus terminals, and baggage lockers, none of which had anything to do with heroin trafficking. The informant even produced a baggage locker key and other information that was easily verifiable and gave the scheme the appearance of being a very good case. As Monday came around, things were not adding up and the informant disappeared when he was needed most. Things really got unraveled when a supervisory agent from the Baltimore office asked to see the informant's photograph. The informant was a fugitive from an ongoing investigation in the Baltimore office. Had the fingerprints been delivered as required, a quick check would have nabbed a fugitive and saved hundreds of wasted investigative hours. The fugitive was eventually arrested and prosecuted but not for furnishing false information to Federal agents. It would have been embarrassing.

RESTRICTING THE USE OF CERTAIN PERSONS AS INFORMANTS

To protect the integrity of your department and investigations, certain persons should be given even closer scrutiny before using them as informants. Particular attention should be given to persons who have a history of violence. You must ask yourself if the information you receive is worth the risk you are taking. Individuals in the following categories are considered more of a risk:

- Persons with many arrests.
- Minors (Will you need written consent of the parent?)
- Persons on parole or probation.
- Drug or alcohol addicts.
- Persons who have been informants in the past and proven themselves to be unreliable.
- Anyone with a perjury conviction.
- Persons with a history of mental illness.
- Persons who are informants for another agency. (Close coordination required.)
- Persons who are in the United States illegally.
- Persons who are prisoners as a result of conviction or who are awaiting trial.

- Persons who have any history of violence, specifically assaults on law enforcement officers.
- Persons who are under any type of restraining order.

It is advisable that a supervisor in your department approve high-risk informants.

The level of approval in the command structure for the use of these persons should match the risk involved. In extremely risky cases, someone higher in the chain of command may be the person who approves the use of a certain informant.

EXAMPLE

Agents were working with an informant who they knew to be an alcoholic. The informant arranged to meet with targets of an investigation at a nightclub where alcohol was served. During the meeting, the informant drank too much alcohol and got involved in an automobile accident resulting in a death. The family of the accident victim sued the department because the informant was an "agent" of that department at the time of the accident. The department was found liable and had to pay a substantial sum of money to the victim's family.

Was there a supervisory review of the use of this informant? Why did the agents allow the informant to arrange a meeting where they knew alcohol was available? The use of certain informants should be restricted. Management must recognize the liability of using certain persons as informants. This situation is a question of control and supervisory oversight.

This page intentionally left blank.

CHAPTER 2

SETTING UP THE INFORMANT FILE

The informant files should be in one location, preferably a file cabinet with a combination lock. The informant should be assigned a random code number. The informant numbers should not be sequentially assigned to avoid any possibility of being identified. An informant logbook with a record of the number and true name, should be maintained in the same safe.

Considering that the informant's name is now on file, access to informant files should be strictly limited to persons with a need to know. The identity of persons with access and the time frame of their access should be documented in a logbook or by memorandum.

Because the informant files should be available anytime, more than one person should have access.

The following information should be in each informant file:

- Identification documentation including fingerprints, photographs, personal history information, and printed results of drivers license, NCIC, and fingerprint check (This documentation should be periodically updated, especially the NCIC check once an FBI number is known)

- Copies of all reports of investigation that mention informant (by their assigned code number) to include reports that contain information obtained because of informant's information or undercover activity (This is to include but is not limited to debriefing reports, undercover reports, arrest reports, and surveillance reports)

- Any statements signed by the informant

- Receipts for reward, expenses, or undercover purchases signed by the informant

- The original signed informant agreement

Some informants have been involved in crime but have never been arrested. The possession by police of this personal data, including the photo and fingerprints, could someday serve the same purpose as an arrest record.

A court may some day order a police department to produce records of the informant's cooperation. This record is usually reviewed privately by a judge to decide if it has any relevance to the case. Having a centralized record system makes court compliance easy.

Internal Affairs investigators should have immediate access to any informant record when an informant makes an accusation against an officer. The record serves many purposes and should never be discarded.

CHAPTER 3

INFORMANT STATEMENTS

PREPARATION & FORMAT OF INFORMANT STATEMENTS

Informant statements should be taken as a debriefing report. That is, the officer should question the informant and prepare a report that is not read, or adopted verbatim, by the informant. Having the informant read your report may impact how the courts handle it. There is no need for the informant to read your report; just paraphrase the information to the informant for accuracy. The prosecutor is the person who must deal with this matter; therefore, you should discuss informant statements with the prosecutor.

Informants should be required to sign some statements. The statements should not be detailed, but sufficient to protect an officer. This type of statement will usually involve the exchange of money or drugs such as an undercover operation. Requiring the informant to sign a statement in this situation will help prevent the informant from stealing or accusing the officer of stealing.

An example of a signed informant statement:

"On March 30, 1999, Officer Grimes, in the presence of Officer Smith, gave me $100. I used the $100 to purchase one gram of cocaine from _____ on the same day, and after making this purchase, I gave the cocaine to Officer Grimes as witnessed by Officer Smith."

Signed by: _____

Date: _____

Witnessed by: _____

Witnessed by: _____

The officer's debriefing report will cover the specific events as they relate to the undercover purchase. The informant should not be permitted to prepare this report. An example:

At about 10:00 p.m. on March 30, 1999, CS-00000 (informant's confidential number), was debriefed regarding the CS' meeting with John DOE.

CS-00000 stated that he arrived at John DOE's residence at 123 Peachtree Street, Atlanta, GA, at about 8:00 p.m. on March 30, 1999. DOE's wife TERESA admitted the CS. DOE was at the kitchen table counting a large sum of paper currency. The CS observed that most of the money was in $20's and the CS estimated there was about $3,000-4,000.

DOE asked the CS what the CS wanted. The CS told DOE that he wanted a "quarter" (one-quarter ounce of cocaine). While the CS waited in the kitchen with TERESA DOE, DOE went to another room at the back of the residence. TERESA DOE asked the CS how the last "quarter" was. The CS responded that it was OK and that the CS sold it right away.

About three to four minutes later, DOE returned to the kitchen and handed the CS a clear plastic zip-lock type bag containing white powder. DOE stated, "The coke is good quality, it has not been cut." DOE told the CS the price was $300. The CS took out $300, money furnished by Detective Grimes, and gave the money to DOE. DOE counted the money and placed it on the kitchen table with the money DOE was counting.

DOE told the CS that the CS could come back anytime. The CS asked DOE if he could furnish up to a kilogram (of cocaine). DOE responded that he would need a day's notice.

The CS then departed DOE's residence and met Detectives Grimes and Jordan at a prearranged location where the CS handed Detective Grimes the cocaine.

Again, this report should not be read verbatim to the informant, rather the facts should be related to the informant to confirm accuracy.

DEBRIEFING THE INFORMANT

Questioning or debriefing the informant should be conducted just as you would question a suspect. That is, none of your questions should contain information. You must remember that the informant could be on an intelligence mission and will repeat whatever you say or ask. For example, a question that contains information:

Do you know Michael GRIMES?

This question lets the informant know that you know Michael GRIMES.

The question should be: Whom do you know in the drug business?

You must analyze every question before you ask it. If the informant insists on being given names because he knows dozens of persons in the drug business, you'll have to wade through all of them until you get to the people you want to talk about.

You must practice the technique of not giving out information. If you hear another officer giving up information during conversation or questioning of an informant, take the officer aside and tell him what he is doing. This could save someone's life.

As the informant mentions names, be careful not to respond verbally or physically. After the informant mentions a name, you must continue by asking race, sex, height, weight, hair color, age, address, vehicles, and any other identifying data. You must do this even if you are positive about whom the informant is talking about.

As I will mention in Chapter 8, you must keep a lid on giving out police information. This is an area where drug officers often get themselves in trouble with informants. Informants sometimes have a cocky attitude about knowing more than the police. They will display this attitude trying to get the officer to show his knowledge. No matter how tempting, do not fall for this trap. Never brag to an informant about what you know, whom you know, whom you are targeting, or who you intend to arrest. Informants who are trying to trap you into giving out information will themselves reveal information. Do not debate them, do not try to outdo them, do not be a fool. An informant will learn very quickly if you are going to give out information. If you do, you will lose the informant's respect and you will lose control.

CORROBORATING INFORMANT STATEMENTS

Corroborating an informant's statements has a twofold purpose. It establishes the informant's truthfulness, and it locates and identifies an evidence trail. Although you will not tell the informant exactly what you do to corroborate his statement, you must let the informant know that you are checking his story. If the informant knows you will be investigating support for his statement, he will be more likely to be truthful.

Some examples of corroborating an informant's statement:

(A) An informant states he knows someone. If the informant knows the target, the informant will know a physical description, address (or at least the city of residence), telephone or pager number, type of vehicle, employment (if any), how the informant met the target and through whom, and the target's associates. Most, if not all, of this information can be easily corroborated through an independent investigation. The informant should be able to give a description of how to get to the target's residence. The telephone number may be in a telephone book or obtainable with a subpoena. The vehicle described by the informant may be parked at the target's residence and it may be registered to the target. You may know the target and will know the informant is telling the truth as the statement progresses. Do not agree to, or acknowledge anything the informant says; act as though you have never known the information.

(B) An informant states he went to another city to transact a drug deal. How did the informant travel—air, bus, train, or automobile? Your investigation may reveal ticket receipts, gas receipts, traffic tickets, hotel records or the location of an overnight stay. Did any unusual event occur during the trip? A television event, sports event, accident, severe weather report, or news report could trigger the informant's memory of the specific day. Drug traffickers are well known to take photographs during parties or outings; these are often found during searches of residences.

(C) An informant states he had long distance telephone conversations with targets or was present when a target made the calls to transact a drug deal. The records are available with a subpoena.

Obtaining corroborative evidence of an informant's statement is only limited by the officer's imagination.

EXAMPLE

A truck was stopped by police in a coastal community and found to contain 12,000 pounds of marijuana. Several weeks later the driver agreed to cooperate. He told agents that the marijuana came from the off-load of a mothership which contained 30,000 pounds of marijuana. The information furnished by the defendant/informant was voluminous; this is a sampling of the corroboration. The informant described the ocean as "slick calm" that night. The national weather service furnished weather records that described the winds as "calm" and the seas as slight waves. The informant stated that four fiberglass boats off-loaded the mothership in one trip. The boats were found as described by the informant and can carry 8,000-10,000 pounds each, depending on the height of the waves. The primary target of the investigation was identified as the purchaser of the boats. The informant stated that one of the rental trucks hit a low hanging oak tree branch on the dirt road leading to the shore side off-load site. The rental company confirmed the rental of the trucks, one of which was returned with damage to the top of the cargo box. The tree with a damaged branch was found and had pieces of the plywood box liner imbedded in the bark.

There were hundreds of other pieces of evidence used during this investigation. Most of the evidence was found using informant information. If you do not check out these statements, be assured a sharp defense attorney will and you and the prosecutor will appear foolish at best.

EXAMPLE

A defendant/informant told agents he had been working as a courier delivering cocaine from Miami, Florida, to North Carolina. During these trips the informant stated he resided at a Miami Springs hotel. Agents could not find the hotel record and went back to the informant. The informant stated he might have used another name. He was then removed from jail with a court order and taken to Miami to find the exact room. It was the agents' intention to find the registration card and match the informant's handwriting. Upon arrival at the hotel, the informant announced he had been lying and had never been to the hotel. It is incredible that an informant would continue the charade knowing he was being taken on an 800-mile trip to find a hotel room. The informant never testified nor was he ever used again. Your trust of an informant should be limited to that information that can be corroborated.

CHAPTER 4

MAKING PROMISES

Making promises about an informant's case or paying a certain amount of reward money can place an officer or department in a position of jeopardy.

The disposition of a defendant/informant's court case is not the province of a police officer or the police department. This is to be decided by the court or by an agreement made between the defendant, the defendant's attorney, the prosecuting attorney and the court. While the police may have some input into the disposition of the defendant/informant's case, the police officer should have no conversation with a defendant/informant about the disposition of the case.

If an officer wants to have input into the disposition of an informant's case, then this conversation should be between the officer and the prosecuting attorney outside the presence of the informant. When an officer makes a representation to an informant about a case disposition, this representation may become binding on the prosecutor. An officer is an agent of the government, and although the officer may not be specifically empowered to make promises about case dispositions, this does not mean that the promise will not become binding. Anything you say may be construed by the hopeful defendant to be a promise. You should affirmatively remind the defendant often that you cannot and will not make promises about his case. Keep in mind that the informant may be wearing a tape recorder anytime you are having a conversation. You or your department could become the target of a lawsuit for breach of contract.

Another area to avoid is promises about specific amounts of reward to an informant. Never set any specific percentage based upon the amount of drugs seized, the value of drugs seized, or the value of property seized such as real property, vehicles, vessels, aircraft, or cash. You never know what you will seize. For example, if you are foolish enough to promise an informant a 10% reward on cash seized and you seize $10,000,000.00 cash, what will you do? Do you think any informant is entitled to a $1,000,000 reward for a few hours or a few days work? The government officials, to whom the head of your department answers, will not think so.

The best policy is never to promise an informant anything about his case or about a reward.

EXAMPLE

Within a few hours of his arrest a defendant agreed to cooperate with agents. The informant was most concerned with what prison sentence he would receive. The agents thought this was the key to getting the defendant to cooperate and engaged in a conversation with the defendant about sentences imposed in similar cases. The agents told the defendant that his sentence could be anything from probation to a short incarceration term. On sentencing day, the U.S. District Court Judge asked the defendant if anyone had made promises about sentencing. The informant recalled what he wanted to recall and told the judge that the agents had promised him probation. The sentencing hearing was promptly postponed and the judge ordered the U.S. Attorney to learn what, if anything, the agents told the defendant/informant. The matter was eventually resolved. This was an embarrassment to the agents. Sentencing matters are exclusively up to court and court officers. Agents should never talk to defendants about sentencing or anything else that may happen to the defendant in court.

This page intentionally left blank.

CHAPTER 5

INFORMANT RELATIONSHIP

MEETING WITH THE INFORMANT

An officer should never meet with an informant alone, including within your office. The only exception to this is when an informant is working in an undercover situation with an undercover officer. The only way to avoid an informant later saying what you may or may not have done or said is to always have a witness.

An officer should maintain a permanent written record of all informant contacts. If an informant calls on the telephone, a written record of the call is necessary. This can be as simple as making a note in your notebook indicating the date and time of the call, and what was discussed. If an officer conducts a debriefing of an informant, a report of investigation should be prepared.

The only conversation that should take place between an officer and an informant is the business conversation. That is, the only topic of discussion should be the informant giving the officer information. Officers should not have personal conversations with informants. An informant is not an officer's friend. This is a business relationship and should be conducted accordingly. Additionally, never make comments to an informant about how cases are progressing or what the department's intentions may be regarding any investigation.

Always remember that during any meeting or conversation with an informant, the informant may be recording the conversation.

We can always control our own behavior, but we cannot always control the behavior of an informant.

EXAMPLE

An informant who had been involved in off-loading tons of marijuana from motherships to shore in the Carolinas cooperated to avoid indictment. The agent met the informant alone several times to obtain information that resulted in several multi-ton marijuana seizures. During this time, the informant continued to conduct his own off-load operations while giving up his criminal associates. The informant was caught in his scheme and was indicted. Trying to diminish his culpability, the informant contacted internal affairs and told investigators that he had been bribing the agent to avoid arrest. The informant then jumped bail and disappeared. The agent was left behind to face the allegation of accepting bribes.

Why was the agent meeting alone with the informant? The only people who know what occurred were the agent and the informant who was no longer available. The agent faced this situation alone. He had no witness. The agent's polygraph was inconclusive which resulted in an unfavorable perception by internal affairs. Although the agent was eventually cleared of any illegal act, his life became miserable and his work product diminished considerably. Both the agent and agency were harmed.

This entire situation could have been easily avoided by not meeting with the informant alone. Agents may not always be able to control the informant, but they can control their own behavior.

DEVELOPING FRIENDSHIPS

An informant is not an officer's friend. A character flaw or perversion is the motivation behind a person becoming an informant. He is someone who has broken a trust although that trust may have been an illegal one with a criminal associate, friend, lover, or family member. Trust is trust; it does not matter if it was for an illegal or immoral act. Officers must recognize the informant for what he is no matter how friendly the informant acts toward the officer. There is no room for friendship between the officer and an informant.

An officer should always act professional and courteous toward an informant. This is imperative, as it will determine if the informant respects the officer. The informant must have a clear understanding of the business nature of the relationship. The person in control of the relationship will determine the direction of the relationship. Officers have what the informant wants; therefore, officers control the relationship.

Once an officer develops a friendship with an informant, the relationship ceases to be professional and the officer may lose some necessary control and respect. This is probably one of the most dangerous areas of the relationship between the officer and the informant. This is historically the area where trouble begins, and an officer's career ends, or a lawsuit begins.

Why would an officer develop a friendly relationship with someone whom he knows cannot be trusted? Officers do not do this in their personal lives nor should they do this in a situation in which their life or career may be at stake.

The officer must guard against developing feelings of emotional affinity with the informant. That is, the officer must never cross the line beyond any natural liking for the informant. If an officer develops an emotional affinity with the informant, it could easily lead to the officer becoming the informant's "protector." The officer may feel he has a personal "stake" or investment in the informant and place too much faith or confidence in the informant. Additionally, an officer who becomes an informant's "protector" may become the target of an informant's street bragging that the informant has an officer in his "pocket." It does not matter that this is not true; what matters is the appearance that the officer has done something wrong or illegal. Many internal affairs investigations have as much to do with perception as with reality. The officer must always remember that he has limited control over an informant outside his presence.

DEVELOPING A RAPPORT

Although the previous Section advises against developing friendships with informants, the officer should be concerned with developing a proper rapport with the informant. Establishing clear rules and guidelines for the relationship develops good working rapport. The informant must know and follow those rules and be clear about the consequences of violating the rules. Similarly, the officer must follow the rules as discussed herein. Knowing that the officer WILL follow those rules without fail is important for the informant. The best working relationships occur when both or all parties know their expected roles and those of others with whom they must function.

EXAMPLE

This example may not be directly related to developing rapport, however, it points to informants not having any loyalty to anyone, least of all an officer. An agent was assigned to handle an informant who was a witness in a pending trial. The agent was directed to maintain a weekly contact with the informant to ensure the informant's continuing cooperation and intent to testify. The agent developed a civil rapport with the informant and met the informant in the office several times. There was no indication of any trouble from this informant. The informant testified, then went about his business having no further contact with the agent.

The agent was later assigned to investigate a dangerous PCP manufacturing organization in which the informant was involved. The agent became a danger to the organization because they knew he was going to succeed because of his determination and perseverance. The head of the organization believed the only way to save himself was to kill the agent; the informant was hired and never tried to warn the agent. On the contrary, intent on murder, the informant began stalking the agent. The informant stalked the agent for two weeks but never had an opportunity. When a member of the organization realized the other members really intended to murder the agent, he became frightened and contacted the agent directly. The agent, now aware of the informant's intent, became vigilant. A few days later the informant was caught stalking the agent, was arrested, convicted, and sentenced to a lengthy prison sentence.

Rapport may be developed, but never a friendship or a relationship of complete trust.

CHAPTER 6

USE OF TAPE RECORDERS

DURING THE INTERVIEW

There may be occasions where tape recording an interview with an informant is advisable. Any tape recordings of the informant will become discoverable by the defense, therefore the decision whether to record should be discussed beforehand with the prosecuting attorney. If there is to be a recording, great care should be taken to explain to the informant the need for accuracy and honesty in the interview.

WORKING UNDERCOVER

If an undercover agent is not present, the only way to ensure the nature of the conversation between an informant and a target/defendant is to record the conversation. Taping can be accomplished in several ways: (a) using a tape recorder worn by the informant, (b) *using a tape recorder planted in a room or inside a vehicle, or (c) using a body wire transmitter and making a recording at the listening post.

There are times when an informant just cannot wear a recorder or body wire transmitter due to the possible danger of discovery. In this situation, every effort should be made to introduce an undercover agent.

If you do not already know your state's laws about using an informant to record, be sure to check with a prosecuting attorney.

*(You must ensure that if the informant [consenting party] is not present in a room or vehicle while a recording is being made, that the recording is not listened to or its contents acted upon. When the informant departs a room where a tape recorder is planted and recording, a consenting party is no longer present. You are then recording without consent, which requires a court order. This is against the law. You must ensure that the informant, the consenting party, remains in the room.)

IS THE INFORMANT TAPING YOU?

During all meetings with an informant an officer must assume that the informant is taping the conversation, whether the conversation is taking place over the telephone or in person.

Many officers assume that the informant's original intent in taping the officer is to trap the officer or to "get something" on the officer. This is the result; it is not the original reason. A defendant/informant will tape an officer because the informant does not trust the officer. That is, the informant is afraid that when he gets to court his cooperation will not be presented to the court as he thinks it should be. From the informant's viewpoint this is reasonable behavior.

An officer should have no fear of the informant taping conversations because the officer should be having no conversations with an informant that cannot be repeated in open court. This taping happens very often; however, it is rarely discovered because informants usually get more consideration in court than they deserve. The tapes are discovered, however, when something happens that is not to an informant's liking; such as and arrest, a long prison term, or a reward that is smaller than the informant expected.

Historically, these tapes have been more embarrassing than anything. Officers who have been taped and embarrassed have usually spoke badly about their coworkers or supervisors.

An officer should never have a conversation with an informant that he is not prepared to have repeated in court, in the media, to his supervisors, or to family members.

EXAMPLE

An agent frequently talked to an informant about matters that did not relate to police business. During these conversations, the agent made less than professional remarks about his supervisor and fellow agents. Following a sentencing that did not please the informant, the informant contacted internal affairs and told the investigators that the agent had made promises about what was going to happen in court. The informant alleged that the government was bound by the agent's comments. As it turned out, the agent did not make any comments that would be binding on the US Attorney. However, the agent did make several unprofessional comments about his supervisor and one other agent. These comments may have been an innocent attempt to win the informant's confidence. The agent was transferred and his reputation followed him. This is not a comfortable position in which to find yourself. Agents must follow the basic rule of never saying anything in the presence of an informant that you are not prepared to state publicly.

CHAPTER 7

USING INFORMANTS FOR UNDERCOVER OPERATIONS

THE DEBRIEFING

Prior to any operation, the informant should be thoroughly debriefed and a report prepared regarding the target or targets of an investigation. The following information should be obtained from the informant about targets:

- Name or alias.
- Physical description of targets.
- Where target resides and frequents.
- Where target works.
- Does informant know if target has ever been arrested?
- I.D. vehicles operated by the target.
- What is target's telephone and pager number?
- How does informant know the target?
- What drugs and in what amounts does the target deal?
- Does informant know target's drug supply source... and how does informant know this?

- Is the target violent or has the target made any threats?

- Will target search for tape recorders or other electronic devices?

- What does informant know about target's method of operation?

- How will the deal go down... what has the informant personally observed or heard?

- Has the target ever conducted counter surveillance?

- Where does the target store drugs?

- Where does the target store cash proceeds?

- What assets does the target possess that were derived from drug trafficking and how does informant know this?

- Can the informant introduce an undercover agent? If not, why not? (Race is not a sufficient excuse.)

- Will the target expect the informant or undercover officer to use drugs?

- What street jargon does the target use for various drugs?

- Does the informant owe the target money... if so, what for?

- Has the informant ever burned (cheated) the target on previous deals?

- Does the target carry weapons... if so, what type?

These are just a sampling of questions an informant should be asked.

Be cautious during this operational debriefing not to reveal information to the informant. As stated in Chapter 3, Section 2, "Debriefing the Informant," none of your questions should contain information.

By example, in question #6 concerning vehicles operated by the target, your question should not be, "Is the target still driving the red Ford?" Your question should simply be "What vehicle(s) does the target own?" Officers should practice this questioning technique until it becomes natural.

CONTROLLING THE INFORMANT WITH SPECIFIC INSTRUCTIONS

Working Undercover with an Informant

If an informant has been properly handled up to this point, there will be no question about controlling an informant while working undercover, either alone or with an undercover officer. The informant must understand that the success of any operation is the responsibility of the police; the informant's responsibility is to follow instructions if they are within the law and within reason.

Before any operation, an informant must be given simple, clear, and concise instructions. These instructions should come from one officer, preferably the undercover officer, not several officers telling the informant what to do. Too many supervisors cause confusion for the informant.

Although an informant is not to be allowed to control the operation, the informant's ideas or opinions should not be ignored. After all, the informant usually knows more about the target than do the officers. You do not have to implement the informant's ideas, but you should consider them before coming up with a final plan.

Some things an informant needs to know before an operation:

- Who is driving, the informant or the UC officer
- What vehicle is going to be used
- Where is the meeting to take place
- How is the informant supposed to introduce the UC
- What is the informant to say about how the informant met the UC and how long has the informant known the UC
- What is the informant supposed to say to the target
- What amount of drugs are going to be purchased or what is the purpose of the meeting
- What prices have been quoted to the informant
- When is the informant to cease taking part in conversation between the UC and target
- As the deal progresses, what is the informant's role (Avoid or limit having the informant handle the money or possess the purchased drugs.)
- Is the informant supposed to depart with the UC
- Have any undetectable signals been worked out between the UC and the informant
- Is there a danger signal the informant can use to alert the UC to danger
- If an arrest is to take place, what are the informant's instructions in this regard

Officers should not limit themselves to these considerations; they are a guide to reason.

MAKING THE INFORMANT PURCHASE

If you do not thoroughly search an informant prior to any undercover operation he may conceal something from you (firearms, drugs, money, other contraband).

Once again, the informant must be thoroughly debriefed prior to making an undercover purchase, and he must be given specific instructions.

First, the informant must be strip-searched. That is, the informant must remove his or her clothing in the presence of two officers of the same sex. The clothing must be thoroughly searched for drugs, weapons, money, or other contraband. The informant's body must be closely viewed for hidden contraband including the rectum, armpits, bottoms of feet, etc. This will ensure that the informant has not hidden anything and cannot be accused of planting evidence.

Next, the informant's vehicle must also be thoroughly searched for the same reason.

The informant is then equipped with a recording or transmitting device and given instructions on its use.

Operational instructions given to the informant should be clear and concise, and these instructions should come from only one officer to avoid confusing the informant. If an officer other than the controlling officer has a recommendation or instruction for the informant then this information should be given to the controlling officer. The controlling officer will then relay the information to the informant. This is a very important point. More than one supervisor could confuse the informant. An informant who does not have a clear understanding of his instructions could place an undercover officer or the informant in danger.

The informant's photograph is to be shown to surveillance officers or the informant can be viewed in a line-up room. The informant should never be brought into a briefing room where the informant can view the officers. The informant has no business knowing the identities of any officers other than the controlling officers and possibly a supervisor. Nor should the informant attend a briefing, as he has no need to know how operations are being planned. Remember that today's informant may be tomorrow's target and will use what he learned against you.

The informant needs to know where to go to meet the controlling officers after a purchase has been completed.

A surveillance team must be in position to follow the informant to the suspect's location. They should attempt to observe the meeting or observe the informant enter and depart the suspect's residence. The informant should then be followed away from the meeting to a prearranged location.

At the prearranged meeting, evidence and technical equipment should be taken from the informant immediately. The informant should then be strip-searched again. A detailed statement should be taken from the informant.

It is recommended that the informant sign a statement, however brief, regarding money given to the informant by officers, from whom the informant made the purchase, and what the informant did with the drugs and any unspent buy money. Specific detail should be recorded in the debriefing report prepared by the controlling officer. As stated earlier, the informant is not an officer and may leave out important details if allowed to write a report of events.

EXAMPLE

A professional informant (working for monetary reward) was recruited to purchase drugs from employees of a large company that was closely associated with the Federal Government. Unknown to the agents, the informant made an agreement with a criminal associate who agreed to play the role of the targets of the investigation. The agents did equip the informant with a body wire transmitter and sent him into the company with buy money. There was no surveillance once the informant departed the agents' presence. The informant was not searched before and after each deal. The informant, who had been given a janitorial job at the company, entered the back of the building and met his friend on the loading platform. The friend, using a name previously given him by the informant, sold the informant drugs at inflated prices. The informant then gave agents a false name for the identity of the person from whom he made the purchase. The body wire transmitter produced poor tapes that were mostly garbled. The informant and his friend profited several thousand dollars from this scheme. About thirty employees were arrested amid publicity. Some employees admitted to using drugs but all denied they ever sold any drugs. After several employees took polygraphs and passed, the informant was confronted. The informant admitted what he had done and then turned his attention on the agents. The informant accused the agents of improprieties during the obviously shoddy investigation. The result was as follows: The informant was charged and convicted of drug distribution, the two case agents were fired, a supervisor was demoted and transferred, and the agency was embarrassed publicly. The thirty employees sued the agency and company for reinstatement and compensation for their wrongful arrest. The company and agency were ordered by the court to compensate each employee with a sum of money that has not been revealed.

EXAMPLE

As recently as 1999, a major eastern city lost a lawsuit involving negligence in the death of an informant. The jury awarded the family of the informant $98 million! The informant had gone to the police with information that he had overheard conversation on a multiple homicide. The informant had been inside a residence where drugs were being sold. The police gave the informant a tape recorder, some buy money, and instructed him to return to the residence. The informant was instructed to make a drug purchase and attempt to get a recording of conversation about the murder. The officers did not attempt to follow the informant. When the informant arrived in front of the residence, he was attacked, beaten and left bleeding on the sidewalk. The informant was still alive when his attackers departed. The informant lay on the sidewalk for 40 minutes and bled to death. You are just as responsible for protecting an informant as you are to protect your fellow officer.

UC LOCATIONS WHEN USING AN INFORMANT

The following locations should not be used during undercover operations that involve informants:

- The informant's residence.
- The informant's place of business.
- The informant's automobile.
- Any location specifically selected by the informant without consultation with the officers.

This is not to say that the informant cannot make suggestions. Allowing the informant to select the meeting location is giving the informant control.

Not only will the informant be familiar with these locations, so will the targets. The more that the targets know about the meeting location the more opportunity they have for using violence against an undercover officer or the informant.

EXAMPLE

An undercover agent met with targets of an investigation at an informant's place of business. The layout of the business was very familiar to the targets of the investigation, as they had been there often. Although they had a mapped layout, the surveillance team and the undercover agent had never been inside the business. It was the intention of the targets to rob and kill the undercover agent; they did not know he was an agent. The targets did in fact murder the agent and severely wound the informant. Two of the targets were captured; the third is a fugitive. This is a situation that was probably unavoidable; however, the question remains whether they would have murdered the agent if they were in an unfamiliar area. In this situation, the surveillance team could not have saved the agent even if they knew the exact layout. It was a question of the targets being comfortable with their surroundings. Sometime all the precautions available cannot save an agent's life.

CHAPTER 8

INFORMANT'S KNOWLEDGE OF POLICE OPERATIONS

When officers become friendly with an informant, they have inappropriate conversations with the informant about many things including police operations. As mentioned earlier, this is historically the beginning of an inappropriate relationship with an informant and the potential for danger or the end of a police officer's career.

Specifically this means that an officer may begin believing he can trust an informant and telling the informant about what is going on seems fine. Some officers may enjoy telling persons in the criminal underworld (their informants) about how criminals are being outwitted. This gives an officer a feeling of power and recognition. To this end, bragging to an informant is the next best thing without violating the law.

Under no circumstance should an officer engage in any conversations with informants about police operations, police methodology, the intended targets of the police, or anything that the informant has no business knowing.

As mentioned in previous chapters, none of your questions to the informant should contain information.

EXAMPLE

Two informants who were working to eliminate competition and avoid prosecution were given free access to the narcotics' office area. The informants overheard conversations and could observe documents. Foolishly, the officers talked to the informants about whom they were investigating and who they anticipated arresting. The fact that the informants were working for the police became known in the criminal community. Trying to lessen their problems with other suspects, the informants told criminals that the police were "on the take." To prove their assertions, the informants predicted arrests and searches.

When the informants were arrested for drug trafficking, the first thing they did was turn on the officers who were controlling them. The informants told internal affairs investigators that the officers were taking money for information. The informants could establish the information side of the story but failed on the money part. Perception overshadowed reality and encouraged the internal affairs officers to believe the informants. The informants failed polygraph questions about paying officers money but passed on getting the information. When the case against the informants went to trial, they got on the witness stand

and told the jury that they had been framed and accused the officers of being corrupt. Although the jury believed the officers, the entire situation was an embarrassment and could have been easily avoided. The officers had no business allowing the informants in the office nor should they have engaged in any type conversation in the presence of the informants.

This page intentionally left blank.

CHAPTER 9

DOCUMENTING INFORMANT PAYMENTS & TAXES OWED

Any money paid to an informant for reward or for reimbursement of expenses must always be well documented, witnessed by two officers, and signed for by the informant.

The informants' payment voucher or record of payment to an informant should contain the following information:

- Case or investigation number
- Payment date
- Payment amount
- Name and signature of officer making payment
- Name and signature of officer witnessing payment
- Name, code number, code name, and true name of informant receiving payment and date payment received by informant
- Informant's signature

- Name and signature of supervisor approving payment
- Informant's initials next to amount of money to acknowledge receipt
- Reason for payment, i.e., reward, expenses, services

This document should be prepared using at least two pages and carbon paper (or fanfold). This is so that the informant is only required to sign the last page that is placed in his file. Your accounting department and the investigative file use the first page that does not identify the informant. The investigative file copy shows how much money was expended on the case. It also alerts the prosecutor that an informant was used on the investigation and how much money was paid to him.

Under no circumstances should an informant be given moneys for which he refuses to sign. An informant who refuses to sign for money is not being properly controlled. Officers should not be permitted to sign a voucher for payments to an informant without the informant also signing. Not getting an informant's signature for money leaves the officer open to dispute with the informant or a defense attorney about how much money the informant received.

Informants may be liable for income taxes due for any money paid and should be informed about this obligation. A statement to this effect should appear on the informant's payment voucher, i.e., "I understand I may be liable for income taxes for money paid to me by the_____Police Department."

EXAMPLE

An informant who was working for money was also dealing drugs. The controlling officer paid the informant without using a voucher system that required the presence of two agents. The informant was arrested by another department and immediately accused his controlling agent of taking kickbacks from informant payments. The informant knew there were no witnesses or a voucher system requiring signatures. From the informant's view, making the accusation was an easy way to cooperate with prosecutors and receive consideration from the court. Although the truth was eventually determined, the officer had to suffer through the investigation and humiliation of being accused of taking kickbacks.

Why was there no voucher system? Why was the officer permitted to make payments to an informant without a witness? This situation could have been easily avoided by using a standardized voucher system that requires the presence of two officers, their signatures, and the informant's signature.

This page intentionally left blank.

CHAPTER 10

INFORMANTS ON PAROLE OR PROBATION

The informant who is on parole or probation may be breaking the law by associating with known criminals even if working at the direction of police.

To avoid any misunderstanding, or to avoid any violation of the law, it is imperative that departments obtain the prior consent of the parole or probation officer before using this type of informant. This consent should be documented in the informant's file.

There are some probationers whom the courts absolutely do not want associating with drug traffickers for obvious reasons. The informant may be under treatment for alcoholism or drug addiction. If an informant is under court order to avoid targets of your investigation, you may be in contempt of a court order. This situation can be easily avoided by speaking with the probation officer and knowing the informant's conditions of probation or parole.

This page intentionally left blank.

CHAPTER 11

THE RULES

The rules for dealing with informants are based upon the misfortune of officers who have been dealing with informants throughout history. The rules are no different from an officer's firearm, badge, bulletproof vest, seatbelt, or any other device used by officers to protect them from harm. An officer would never go out to make an arrest without at least a firearm and vest. So why would a drug officer not implement The Rules into everyday life for protection?

The Rules are simple and easy to follow. Most of the rules for working with informants include things we do in our everyday lives. None of the rules are violations of the law.

THE RULES

1. An informant is not your friend.

2. You will have no business dealings with an informant.

3. You will never meet an informant alone; this includes your office.

4. You will make a written record of all informant contacts and meetings.

5. You will not make any promises about an informant's case, nor will you make any promises of reward.

6. You will not give an informant your home telephone number or tell an informant anything about your personal life.

7. You will strip-search an informant before and after each operation. If you do not do so, the informant may conceal something from you (drugs, money, weapons, and evidence).

8. Assume during all conversations with an informant that you are being tape recorded, whether in person or on the telephone.

9. You will ensure that an informant's knowledge of police operations is kept to a minimum.

10. Your trust of an informant should be limited only to information you can corroborate.

11. The rules relate to our behavior. We can always control our own behavior; we may not be able to control the behavior of an informant.

EXAMPLE

An informant gave an officer a ball cap (with price tag attached). The informant had a long criminal history of shoplifting. Another officer in the squad complained to the informant that he did not receive a hat. The informant returned later with another hat (with a price tag attached). As the informant's cooperation continued, he began taking orders from the officers for specific items of clothing which were delivered with store tags attached. The officers knew the informant's track record of shoplifting. Every time the informant was arrested, he cooperated by making drug cases.

The officers should have known where the informant was obtaining the clothing. The matter came to the attention of internal affairs when the informant was caught selling a large amount of cocaine to an undercover officer of another department in another city. The informant decided he did not want to face a jail sentence and turned on the officers for accepting the items of clothing. In this case internal affairs officers, with the aid of the informant, set up a sting operation. The officers placed their clothing orders with the informant who was now wearing a wire furnished by internal affairs investigators.

This is a case of officers accepting something of value from an informant. The continuing acceptance of gifts was inexcusable and constituted criminal acts. The officers knew the informant was a shoplifter. Why did the officer accept any gift from the informant in the first place? This entire situation could have been avoided by refusing to accept the first ball cap. The officers lost their jobs and were charged with crimes relating to receiving stolen goods. This was an enormous price to pay for a ball cap.

EXAMPLE

A state agent recruited a defendant/informant and proceeded to break every "rule." The agent and informant developed a friendly relationship. The informant delivered a load of firewood to the agent's home. The agent invited the informant into his home for dinner and to meet the agent's wife and children. The informant knew the agent's home telephone number, pager number, and became very familiar with the agent's family.

The agent began telling the informant details about the investigation, including targets and police techniques. The informant then began approaching targets of the investigation and convinced them that they should go to the agent to confess and make a deal with the government. The informant even went as far as taking targets to the agent's office where the targets confessed and were then debriefed in the informant's presence. The agent promised the informant that he would do everything possible to get the informant a probationary sentence.

During this entire time, the informant was making tape recordings of his conversations with the agent to ensure that the agent would not double cross him on sentencing day. When sentencing day arrived, the agent testified at length about the fifty-five convictions obtained because of the informant's cooperation. The judge imposed a probationary sentence after suspending an eighty-five year incarceration term. Everyone was happy with the outcome. Until this time, there appeared to be no problem.

About eight months later, the informant was caught in a fencing operation, prosecuted, convicted, and had his eighty-five year sentence from the previous drug conviction reimposed. The informant was no longer happy with his situation. The result was predictable. Although the agent was not found to have committed any crime, the next three years of his life were hellish. He resigned in disgrace. When the informant finished with his accusations, perception and reality were indistinguishable. The agent violated every "rule" in the book; he was vulnerable to whatever accusation the informant made.

It is worth repeating here that we can always control our own behavior, but we may not be able to control the behavior of an informant.

This page intentionally left blank.

CHAPTER 12

LEGAL ISSUES OF MISHANDLING INFORMANTS

One of the most commonly encountered problems in dealing with informants is the inability of officers and agents to maintain adequate control over the informant. Control relates to the relationship established at the outset. The rapport that is developed must be one in which the informant respects the officer and one in which the informant knows his or her limitations. That is, the informant must recognize that his role is to follow instructions that he does not control investigations. Trouble begins when the officer loses control of the informant and the informant takes control of the investigation, they go hand-in-hand. A commonly heard term is that an officer is only as good as his informants. This is better stated as an officer is only as good as his ability to control his informants.

In this example, an informant was recruited by a federal agency during the mid-1980's. Although the informant stated his motivation was to do something about the drug problem, his true motivation was money. He was a mercenary. After fifteen years of work, and earning hundreds of thousands of dollars in reward money, the informant is no longer useful. It is documented that the informant lied under oath on many occasions. The federal agency suffered embarrassment in both the courts and news media because it failed to control the informant.

The informant worked on setting up undercover operations in which a buy-bust occurred. The informant introduced an undercover agent as a drug purchaser, occasionally money was flashed, and an arrest was made when drugs were delivered. On occasion, the informant was called to testify. For this work the informant was paid nominal fees.

As the informant traveled from city to city setting up drug deals, he became involved in more lucrative reverse sting operations. The informant posed as a drug source of supply or introduced an undercover agent as the source. When targets delivered money, they were arrested. The seized money was confiscated, forfeited, and a percentage was paid to the informant as a reward. Naturally, it was to the benefit of the informant to obtain as much money for the drugs as possible.

Following several very successful operations the agents began to allow the informant to be the center of the investigation. The agents also allowed the informant to assume the power and authority of an agent. The agents did this by permitting the informant access to areas in the office other than the informant meeting room. He was taken into the squad room where he was free to wander around and observe the activities of agents. Agents discussed investigations and tactics in the informant's presence.

There is no question that this informant was a valuable element in each investigation. He was good in his ability to sell himself to a street corner dealer as well as a banker. He was a "natural" for being an informant. However, the same assets that made him a successful informant helped him to "con" the agents. He gained their "blind" confidence and trust by always delivering good cases.

As the informant moved from city to city, he dealt with different agents. The informant gravitated to agents who controlled him the least and gave him a loose rein. Outside his cooperation with the federal agency, the informant began to have encounters with local authorities because of unlawful acts. He was arrested for soliciting a prostitute, forgery, making false statements, and impersonating a federal officer. In some instances the agency intervened to have charges dismissed. This intervention by the agency and the continued use of the informant was tantamount to acceptance of the criminal activity by an entity sworn to investigate and prevent criminal behavior.

While these charges did not result in felony convictions, they represented a criminal record. As required by regulation, a criminal history check was performed occasionally on the informant and a record of the arrests, convictions, and declined prosecutions was placed in the informant's file. However, the agency was alleged to have not disclosed to prosecutors the information about this criminal activity by the informant.

As the informant traveled and met agents he naturally wanted to maintain the lucrative relationship he had established with the agents. After all, the agents were paying him hundreds of thousands of dollars. To ingratiate himself with the agents further, the informant provided inappropriate benefits to the agents. When dining out, the informant picked up the "tab," often paying hundreds of dollars for dinners in fancy nightclubs. When the check arrived, the informant quickly took the check and paid the bill before the agents had a chance to offer to pay. There were nights on the town when the informant freely bought drinks for agents. Some agents accepted the informant's friendly and seemingly harmless gestures. As far as the informant was concerned the gestures were harmless and the informant really intended no harm to the agents nor was he setting any agents up for a "fall." This appeared harmless to the agents and was not against the law. What were the agents to do?

During these dinners and nights out, the agents and informant engaged in seemingly harmless and personal conversations. The informant learned about the agents' families, the agents' financial matters, the agents' social life, and personal problems. Agents frequently spoke in the informant's presence and freely talked with the informant about methods of operation, including scripted undercover conversations, methods of electronic tracking, money-laundering, and other investigative techniques. The informant learned too much about the inner workings of a law enforcement agency. An old adage says that the best way to defeat an enemy is to understand them.

One agent who was in financial difficulty borrowed $10,000 from the informant. According to both the informant and the agent the verbal agreement was that the agent could repay the money when he had it, and if he did not have it, the debt could be canceled. The agent took the money and never repaid the informant. Later, the agent was called to testify for him in one of the informant's criminal prosecutions. Because of the agent's testimony, the case was dismissed.

Another agent was having automobile problems with his personal auto and borrowed the informant's Mercedes for a few days while his personal car was being repaired. This agent also was later called to testify in the informant's behalf.

This is an informant whose undercover work and testimony has put more than 200 defendants in prison. Some of these defendants were major drug traffickers and are serving life sentences.

During more than one trial, the informant testified under oath that he did not have any criminal record, and that he had never been arrested. The agency, which was aware of the informant's criminal history, did not correct this testimony. Defense attorneys later found out that the informant did have a criminal record. This informant had lied under oath, plain and simple. The true travesty is that this perjury occurred with the complicity of the agency. Courts of appeal rightly criticized the government and some cases were vacated, while others were sent back for retrial.

Following the public disclosure in courts of appeal that the informant had lied, the agents continued using the informant in other locations rather than forever dropping this informant from the list of acceptable informants. Had this informant engaged in merely one transgression there could have been reevaluation of his usability. However, his continued criminal acts should have forever banned him.

In many cases involving this informant, none of the defense attorneys were informed about the informant's record, specifically about lying to officers that he was a federal agent and convicted of this charge. Prosecutors also learned that the informant was under investigation for income tax evasion. The informant never reported any of the reward moneys on his income tax return. This information was not disclosed to defense attorneys. It is important to note here that not only does a prosecutor have a responsibility to furnish discovery material about informants who are going to testify, the agents have a responsibility to report this information to the prosecutor. Discovery includes not only a criminal history of the informant but also any benefits given to the informant whether as money, help with pending criminal matters, or any other benefit no matter how inconsequential. Providing a carton of cigarettes or a meal to an informant may seem minor, but it must be disclosed.

Are these cases going to be vacated because of the agents' and informant's behavior? Were any agents who knew about the informant's criminal history in the courtroom when the informant testified that he had no criminal record? Of course, the informant had a responsibility to tell the truth. If agents were in the courtroom then they had a responsibility to report that they believed the informant testified falsely. This should have never happened. There should have been a conversation between the prosecutor and agents about any benefits given to the informant, and the informant's record in the very beginning of the prosecution phase of this case.

It is imperative that agents and officers continually remind informants about the necessity and value of always telling the truth. The outcome of all cases must be based upon truthful statements and testimony. The ultimate responsibility of any investigation and prosecution is that of the law enforcement agency and prosecutor. The only responsibility of the informant is to follow instructions and always be truthful with the agency and prosecutor.

The informant in this example is facing prosecution for perjury, failure to pay income taxes and a probable incarceration term. The only possible hope this informant has is again to inform on someone else. Because of the informant's prior perjuries he has no value as an informant in the ordinary case, however, he does hold some "cards" in his information about agents that you can be sure he will "deal." Internal affairs and the prosecutor are duty bound to investigate these allegations. Whether they amount to a prosecution or not, the agents involved will suffer through the investigation of every minute aspect of their lives and relationship with this informant. The only way he can get a sentence reduction is to cooperate with the government in the prosecution of other defendants.

You have read this book you know the potential consequences. As you read this example of informant mishandling, you should have been alerted to each consequence of not only the informant's behavior but also the agent's behavior.

The informant has his evidence to go after the agents; the agents gave it to him every time they violated the Rules.

It matters not whether the agents violated any laws or agency regulations, what matters is the perception of the agents' behavior when they violated the Rules and other standards or common sense practices.

As an investigator handling informants you must live by the Rules until they become second nature. It is a matter of your survival as an officer, and possibly your freedom.

NOTES

NOTES

NOTES

NOTES

NOTES

NOTES